PAIN, PASSION, PURPOSE

PAIN PASSION PURPOSE

BRAD BUTLER II

Pain, Passion, Purpose
Copyright © 2018 by Brad Butler II

ISBN-13: 978-0-578-40626-8
ISBN-10: 0-578-40626-8

This book is dedicated to the memory of:

Pearl "Babe" Kim
Jonathan "Gage" Brown
Celeste Brown-Butler
Charles Butler
Brenda ' Potchie' Calhoun

Family First

Ever since I was young, I've always felt like I've had the weight of the world resting on my shoulders. There was always a sense of duty to protect and provide for my family by any means necessary. Maybe that comes from my father. He's always been a provider—at any cost.

My family has always had ups and downs, but our small circle has managed to stay intact. This small circle consists of my father, Brad Butler Sr., my mother, Gheya Butler, my full-blooded sister, Ciji Butler, and me, Brad Butler II.

CHAPTER 1
Senior

My family and I are all originally from Jersey City, New Jersey. My father was a popular drug dealer; he owned about three blocks. He worked out of nice establishments like pool halls and restaurants, paying off the owners to keep them quiet. My sister and I would stop by the trap house every now and then with our mom to say hi, but my father always would always say, "Gheya, what did I tell you about bringing them kids around here? This ain't no place for kids." And my mother would always reply with, "Butler, shut up."

Everyone in the neighborhood respected my dad. He was raised off the old school rules when it came to the drug game. No selling to the elderly, pregnant women, or kids… and you never get high on your own supply. In the words of a true OG, "That's how you screw up the church's money."

Moving the product was his first priority, but a close second was protecting his territory. It's simple: the more area you control, the more money you make.

My father has had many encounters with people who tried to ease in on his turf. It could be something as small as trying to set up shop on one of his corners, or as big as trying to take over his whole operation. Those people never succeeded. You see, my father was an alpha male, or what my mother would call "a man's man." He stood at 5'8" and weighed 200 pounds—all solid muscle, dark skin, and a fixed expression on his face that read: *I don't know you, I don't want to know you, and if we argue, my first response will be to break your jaw.* And on many occasions, he did. Strong legs and a wide back, I remember my mom hugging my dad and not being able to fit her arms all the way around him. He would always say to me, "Son, you gotta make sure you're in shape just in case someone tries you, then you can crack a brother the right way."

At home and around family, he went by Brad, "Buddy," or just plain Dad. He didn't say it a lot when we were young, but my sister and I always knew he loved us. He would encourage us to do the best we could in school—he had minimal education , so he was dead-set on giving us opportunities he never had.

For the record, I'm fully aware of how much poison and violence my father pumped into the community—and there's no excuse for that—but he was doing what he thought was right to take care of his family. In his mind, he didn't see any other options as a black male living in the inner city—a man who came from a large, poverty-stricken family.

This is why I make sure to put the *II* at the end of my name. I want people to know that I am my father's son and, even though people may have looked down on our name, I have decided to devote the rest of my life to cleaning up that name, not just in Jersey City, but everywhere I go. For every life that was taken due to my father's drug dealing ways, I'm going to motivate, inspire, and empower a thousand times that number to breathe life and positivity into the world.

CHAPTER 2
Big Gheya

My mother has got to be, hands down, the strongest, most resourceful, caring person I know. When I say she is the definition of ride or die, other women could attend her 101 class. A light-skinned slim with an athletic build, she stands at about 5'6" and weighs 150 pounds soaking wet. With her iconic short and blonde curly hair, she was never one to miss an opportunity to show off her Jersey house music dance moves because, in our family, my mother has always set the stage, and dance is her form of expression. You could party all night at a family get together, have Hot 97 wake you up as an alarm clock for school, dance your pain away when times were rough, or get your ass whipped to a *Rocky* soundtrack if you decided to act up at the wrong time. Gheya Butler is everything I ever could have asked for in a mother, and I owe her a debt that can never be repaid. But that won't stop me from trying. A lioness in human form, she's always willing to put her life on the line without thinking twice to protect us. She worked right alongside my father in the drug game. Anything he needed, she could handle. Everything from counting the profit to moving the product, she did it all.

I distinctly remember an incident when Mom and Dad were out doing their normal rounds in the neighborhood one night when, all of a sudden, some jack boy from another state got the drop on them. Whoever it was that hired him knew they had to get someone from out of state, because anybody from New Jersey wouldn't have been able to pull that off with all the lookouts my parents had. You could tell he was a pro—the way he crept up on them and pulled out the gun and said, "All right now, y'all know what this is. Now give it up smooth, and don't make a scene."

"Ain't diss about ahhh?" my father asked.

"Yeah, and don't try to be a damn hero."

But before my father could get another word in, my mother piped up. "If you're gonna shoot him, you're gonna have to shoot me first."

"Gheya, if you don't get yo ass out the way, he got a gun," my dad warned.

"I don't care. If he wants this money, he's gonna have to shoot both of us."

The jack boy knew he had already wasted too much time, and he was hired to catch a lick, not two bodies. All he could say was, "Lady, you effin' crazy."

"Yeah, I know."

Then he took off running. My mom was happy they saved the money, but all my dad could think about was how crazy his lady was.

"Gheya, what the hell is wrong with you?! Don't you ever pull that again. Not over no money. I could easily get that money back. He could have killed us!"

"I know, but he didn't. Now let's go home," she replied.

My father has told me that story a million times, and he always ends it by saying, "And son, I'm gonna tell you, after that, I knew I was gonna marry your mother."

I remember thinking, *Well, goddamn, what was it? A rite of passage to get the ring? I don't know if I'm willing to die for the person I'm trying to marry. Maybe after we get the marriage going strong, but I guess Dad needed to see the proof up front.*

You'd think that situation would be enough excitement for a lifetime—nope. Not for "Big Gheya." We call my mom Big Gheya because of the size of her heart. I've never seen her back down from anyone or anything, even when she knows she could be on the end of a losing battle. If my mother believes wholeheartedly in something, she will fight for it to the end. That's where I get my passion and spirit from when I speak. When I get in my zone, I feel like there isn't a thing in this world that can touch me.

My mother and I, we wear our hearts on our sleeve, we love hard, and when the love is gone, it's gone. In fact, the urge to become a motivational speaker hit me after my mother played a recording of her speaking to a group of people to motivate them and help them get through a tough situation. She was so transparent; she didn't pull any punches. Even though it was only an audio recording, I could close my eyes and picture her standing at the podium, her words laced with passion and conviction, commanding the full attention of her audience, tugging on their heartstrings as they hung on to her every word. After hearing my mother on that CD, I knew for a fact that I had the ability to speak with a power I hadn't tapped into yet, and I knew I needed to find a way to tell my story to the world. I figured if it's in my mother, it's got to be in me too, right?

CHAPTER 3
My Sister's Keeper

My relationship with my older sister, Ciji, is a bond most people will never understand. At five years apart, we act like twins. We can be around each other all day and never get sick of each other. We know how to spend quality time with one other, and we give each other space when needed. We understand each other in a way that only a brother and sister could. Ciji is my ace, my right-hand woman. We will always have a friendship that's different from any of my other friendships because I wasn't always this bold and passionate speaker. She remembers when I was her shy little brother, a boy who would use her body as a shield when girls tried to talk to me. She was the person who helped me build my self-confidence and find my swagger. She has always provided tough love, not really one for sappy declarations and hugs. She prefers to show her love through actions, like cooking full course meals, talking friends and family through their problems, or threatening to punch any girl that even thinks of doing me wrong.

I remember coming home from school one day and I was mad because a girl shot me down when I asked her to be my girlfriend. It felt like my whole six-year-old world came crashing down. We were in our room and Ciji was standing in front of the mirror, brushing her hair. She saw me sitting on the floor, sulking as I played with my toys.

"What's your problem?" she asked.

"Do you think I'm ugly?"

"Look, this ain't *The Brady Bunch*. I don't know if you're looking for somebody to feel sorry for you, but I don't. Why are you asking, anyway?"

I told her I'd asked Deana McClain to be my girlfriend, and she said no. "I think she said no because I'm ugly."

"Well, just because she doesn't like you doesn't mean you're ugly. I know a girl down the block who likes you."

"Oh, okay...." I tried to be chill, but really I was thinking, *Whaaaaaat*?!

Sure enough, Ciji walked me down the street to meet her friend's little sister. I never asked her to be my girlfriend, but it was nice to know that a girl my age thought I was cute.

It wasn't always like that with us. As kids, we would fight over the smallest things. We could say and do whatever we wanted to each other, but if anybody else tried to disrespect one of us, it was about to be a real problem. Despite the fact that we're both protectors, we are vastly different in personality. Ciji is the rebel; she'll do things her way whether you like it or not. You can point her in the right direction and she'll take it from there, but don't expect her to ask for a hand holding or a free pass. She gets through tough times all on her own. As for me, I stayed in line and cruised through childhood. Ciji even gave me the nickname Prince Hakeem—from the movie *Coming to America*—because she insists that growing up, I got whatever I wanted from our parents. It's not that I got whatever I wanted, I just listened to whatever they told me to do.

A ride or die like my mother, they don't make 'em like Ciji anymore. She's the toughest person I know. When I saw her raising a child all on her own, my respect for her solidified. She had my nephew, Sincere, when she was seventeen years old. She did what she had to do on her own—finished high school, worked multiple jobs, and never got any help from the father of her child. I know all the things she had to go through to make the best of her situation, and I greatly admire her for it. Watching her become the woman she is over the years has shown me what it takes to get the job done and, sadly, many single moms don't get the recognition they deserve.

I love you, Ciji, for all that you have done, and all that you continue to do. Thank you for showing me that strength is much more than what most would define it as. Thank you for every sleepless night and exhausting day. For every time you worked your fingers to the bone just to make someone else happy. Thank you for being a pillar of strength, one that everyone in this family can look up to. You're the best sister any guy could ask for.

"CHAPTER 4"
"Potchie"

Even though my grandmother taught me a lot about being a gentleman, she was not without fault. At times, she could be considered a Dr. Jekyll and Mr. Hyde. Brenda Calhoun, also known as "Potchie," was a loving, caring, God-fearing woman who was kind to everyone. Then you had the other side—a woman who struggled with alcohol and drugs. Unfortunately, you never really knew which version you were going to get. She was unpredictable, to say the least. She could go from volunteering at a homeless shelter to getting locked up for outstanding warrants or disturbing the peace.

She stood at about 5'6" and possessed a Native American and African American skin tone. Her wardrobe would be considered unique to most. One outfit that I vividly remember was when I was talking to one of my friends after school and my grandmother came walking down the street wearing a bandana with dollar bills all over it, a Notorious B.I.G. t-shirt, a gray blazer, khaki pants, and brown sandals with a gold nose ring, holding a Colt 45 in a paper bag. As she was walking down the street to meet me, my friend said, "Yo, who is that?" and I remember saying, "Shut up! That's my grandmother."

When she reached us, I introduced the two, then Grams and I were on our way. While walking home, I said, "Dang, Grandma, why you always got to dress like that? It's embarrassing. You could at least match your clothes."

"You know I don't care about the way I dress."

"Yeah, but it's still embarrassing."

"I'm not changing the way I dress because I'm not here to impress these raggedy punks."

That's Grams. One minute she'll be telling you how much she loves you, quoting scriptures from the Bible, then in the same breath, she'll turn around and tell somebody across the street to pay up or else. She would always greet people with a friendly, "Howdy, stranger," or "Hey, cool breeze," then ask a someone walking by if they could loan her a dollar so she could get a loosie from the corner store.

When she was in a good mood, things were great. She would take us out to eat and we'd travel around the city. She was God-fearing; however, she never went to church. She would always tell me that I was given the middle name David in honor of David and Goliath. Although, her nickname for me was "Horseman" or "Old Man of Mine."

The one thing we never had to question was how much she loved us. She would always say, "I love my family and my family comes first. You know if it came down to it, I would kill a rock about you." Sadly, I believe she was unhappy with some of the things in her life, which is why she used drugs and alcohol as a coping mechanism. To this day, my family and I still don't understand how she was able to be a functioning alcoholic and an avid drug user. I had never really known her to hold a steady job, yet she always found a way to make some money here and there. I assume it was beg and borrow, hopefully not steal.

During the times I struggled in school, I remember having to come home every day and read Hooked on Phonics, and I remember those days vividly because, more often than not, I didn't want to go home and study with my grandmother because I didn't know if she had been drinking or using that day. When she hadn't been, we would sit down and go through the books and I would work on spelling, sounding out words, and reading sentences out loud. However, when she had been drinking or using, she had no patience for any mistakes.

Misspelling or mispronunciation would normally end with me receiving a beating via a belt or an extension cord, leaving me with bruises and welts on my legs, back, and arms. My sister was always a good student, so she was able to go out and play when she got home after school. In other words, she was never around when any of this was happening. Sometimes, after I had gotten a beating from my grandmother, I would go downstairs to the bathroom to clean myself up. Aunt Della would hear me crying from the first floor and come get me, then I would finish studying with her. My aunt was a nice, soft-spoken, churchgoing woman. I was always happy when she would come and rescue me. I remember overhearing a conversation one day between my grandmother and my aunt after my grandmother had beaten me. Aunt Della said, "Why do you keep beating him like that? He's never going to learn that way."

"Shut up, Della. It's because he's not paying attention."

For most people, they might read this and think, *oh wow, he must've had a terrible relationship with his grandmother*. It's actually the opposite. I know my grandmother loved and cared for me as only a grandmother could, and it's hard to understand the relationship you have with someone when you know that person is struggling with an addiction. I have forgiven my grandmother for the abuse I received as a child because our good memories far outweigh that short period of time in our history. So, yes, Grandma, I love you—and I'd kill a rock about you too.

CHAPTER 5
Addiction

During the time my father was dealing, both he and my mother developed a heroin addiction. I imagine it happened because he was around drugs so much that, eventually, he broke down and tried some himself. I know for my mom, the stress of the world got to her, so the drugs were an escape.

Now, as you probably know, if you're in the drug game long enough, one of two things will happen: either you will go to jail, or you will die. Unfortunately, my father became incarcerated, which turned out to be a blessing in disguise. When he got out of jail, I was the first person who spoke to him. I didn't fully understand why he left for such a long time, and when I asked why he was gone, he said, "Daddy did a bad thing. He had to go to jail." I begged him not to go again.

After that conversation, he made a conscious decision that many men in the drug game don't ever make: he chose to step away get a regular job and work at nine to five like everybody else. He forfeited fast money for the sake of his family and his own personal well-being. This caused a new kind of stress because he was used to having a whole lot of cash, and now he didn't. To top it off, we also had to deal with my parents' addiction. From the outside looking in, it seemed everybody in the community viewed at us as black sheep. I could almost hear them thinking: *How could this family amount to anything? What good can ever come of this? Look at their situation.*

Thankfully, my parents both decided that they didn't want to let addiction control their lives. My mother started going to go to NA/AA meetings to kick her habit. Sometimes, I would go with her and sit down or sleep on the benches while she shared her experience with the room.

She would talk about how the habit formed, how it impacted her daily life, and how she wasn't going to allow it to destroy her because she realized that addiction wanted her dead and she wanted to be around for our family. I do remember listening to her cry as she would share her story. I didn't fully understand at that time because I was young, but all I knew was that my mother was sad and I wanted to fix it.

My father, on the other hand, was able to beat his addiction without seeking outside help. He essentially stopped cold turkey, and I watched him go through withdrawal, always throwing up and getting sick, my mom stepping in and putting him in the bathtub. Nevertheless, he beat that addiction along with all his others. He stopped smoking and drinking and started lifting weights and shooting hoops to keep his body in shape.

I believe that's part of the reason why I have such a strong work ethic—Dad was always on the move. He was always doing something productive. I rarely saw him lounging around, watching TV. If it was family time, then he'd sit in the house and watch *In Living Color* or *The Cosby Show* with us, but that was always the exception, not the norm.

CHAPTER 6

All We Needed

Even though we dealt with a lot of struggles when I was young, those were probably some of the best times of my life. We didn't have a whole lot of money after my father stopped selling drugs, but we had a lotta love. Dad got a job working for warehouses and became a handyman on the side; he could fix just about anything. I also remember after he quit the drug game, he didn't have a car or a bike to travel to work with every day, but he did anything he could to provide for the family.

I remember those struggles like it was yesterday. The lights being turned off, not having hot water, not having a whole lot of food in the house. I remember eating syrup sandwiches and drinking sugar water. We even had our electricity shut off a time or two. My father climbed an electric poll once to reconnect our power just so I could watch *Power Rangers*. The place we were living in at the time was located on Martin Luther King Drive, right above a corner store. It was a two-bedroom, one bathroom apartment. It was small, but we had everything we needed—each other. And whenever my mom and dad had some extra money, we would go downstairs and buy some candy from the corner store. My favorite things to get: the sweet potato pie cups and Honey Buns.

I remember one time my mom gave me five dollars and I ran downstairs to the corner store and bought five dollars' worth of ten-cent *X-Men* bubble gum because they had the little fake tattoos on them. I came back upstairs with this bag full of gum and dumped them all out on the table…and then Mom appeared.

"Boy, what are you doing with all this candy?!"

"Well, you gave me some money to get whatever I wanted, so this is what I got."

"You bought five dollars' worth of candy?"

"Well, yeah…. I wanted all the tattoos."

Gritting her teeth, she said, "Put it all back in the bag. You're taking it back—NOW!"

Of course, me being a kid, I start complaining and whining because, yes, when I was younger, I was a crybaby. I don't know why, even when someone would call my name with too much bass in their voice, I always thought I was in trouble. It's kind of funny when I think about it. I cried so much when I was younger, I just cried it all out of my system.

I also remember feeling like I had to be the protector whenever we traveled somewhere as a family. I always made sure I was near my mom and sister. I tried to look out for them at all times and make sure nobody was trying to harm them. I paid real close attention when another man was having a conversation with my mom or my sister. Bonus duties included opening the doors for them, taking out the trash, and making sure I always walked on the outside of the sidewalk. It's something my family instilled—to make sure the women were safe at all times.

A common witness to these practices, my grandmother loved to remind me that one day I'd grow up to be a good man. She'd always tell me to be a gentleman and protect my mother and sister. She said I was the man of the house when my father wasn't around, a title I took serious pride in. Unfortunately, I must admit there have been times in my life where I can honestly say that I dropped the ball on being the gentleman. Whenever I make a mistake or a bad decision that betrays my character, it always bothers me. It hurts to go back and think about it, knowing I was capable of more. Being in my family, you had to develop some tough skin, especially if you were male. Sometimes that would get in the way of being a gentleman. However, having a whole lot of female cousins—and one rockin' mom and sister—paid off. I learned to respect women.

I guess that's why I was never the type of guy who could do women (or people in general) wrong and not feel some type of way about it later. I've had situations where I said something I didn't mean, and somewhere along the line, I had to summon the courage and say, "Listen, I apologize for what I said or did. You didn't deserve to be treated that way. I didn't mean it, and I should've handled the situation better. I should've been a better man."

I'm far from perfect, but I know I'm a better man now than I was before. To my late Aunt Babe, I wish you could see the man I've become. When you left us, I finally understood the saying: "Give people their flowers while they're still alive." That's what I try to do every day. Thanks, Aunt Babe. Remember, it's not goodbye. It's, I'll see you later. Love you and miss you.

In Jersey City, I got picked on a lot when I was younger. I was smaller than everybody else, and for a long time, I got mistaken for a girl because I had a ponytail that came down my back. Then as the years passed, my male features started to kick in and everybody took notice. I remember going to school and being around my sister, and all her friends wanted to touch my hair, talkin' about how "cute" I was. "Look how long his hair is. It's so nice," one praised. And another: "Oww, Ciji, he is going to be a little heartbreaker."

Even though it was a hit with the ladies, I wasn't exempt from being bullied by the guys. They would make fun of me and pull my hair. I couldn't stand it. I remember coming home angry one day and my mom and my grandma asked, "What's wrong?"

I told them that I was mad because I got tired of people picking on me.

"Well, what do you want to do about it?"

"I don't know," I said. "I just want them to leave me alone because I feel like they want to fight me, and I don't want to fight."

"Okay, well, here's what we're going to do: we're not going to be going back and forth to school arguing with the principals and teachers about kids that are picking on you, so we are going to take you down to Mr. Dupree's boxing gym and you're going to learn how to box." My grandmother made sure to add, "Yeah, 'cause we ain't raising no punks in this family."

The next day, Grandma signed me up for boxing classes. Every day after school, I walked all the way down to Mr. Dupree's boxing gym. Grandma accompanied me on the very first day. I looked around the gym but didn't see anybody.

Suddenly, Mr. Dupree came walking out the back. He had on jeans with a white shirt tucked into his pants. He had somewhat of a big belly, but he was a really nice guy and he always greeted me with a smile.

From the first day we met, he insisted there was something special about me. I kept thinking, *Okay, let's get started with the training and see how this goes.*

"Okay, well, where are the boxing gloves?" I asked.

"Well, the first thing we're going to do is build up your cardiovascular system."

Now, I was so young, I didn't really know what that word meant.

I said, "What's that?"

"We're going to build up your stamina."

"Oh, okay."

"All right. Here's what you're going to do. You're going to take this jump rope and jump for ten minutes straight. Don't stop until the ten minutes are up. I'll set the timer."

"Okay," I said.

Every day after school, I would come in and work out. Mr. Dupree liked me because I didn't have a problem following instructions. If he asked me to jump rope for ten minutes straight, I would. If he asked me to punch the bag for five minutes straight, I would. If he asked me to spar for two-minute rounds, I would—anything to learn how to protect myself and my family.

Things were going well. I was doing my workouts and, for a short period, nobody picked on me. After a while, Mr. Dupree mentioned that he wanted me to be in the local newspaper. This came as a surprise. I didn't think I was that good of a boxer, but he said I had a lot of potential and that I was smart and showed a willingness to improve. That's something I'll never forget.

It was only going to be a matter of time before people found out that I was boxing at Mr. Dupree's gym and decided that they wanted to test it and see if I could really fight or not.

Up until this point, I hadn't really gotten into any fights—maybe a show fist here or there. I remember getting my food from the cafeteria and setting it down on the table, then running back to get my juice. When I returned to the table, I was trying to find my tray but couldn't. I knew I'd left it right there, but it was nowhere to be found. I started asking around

"Hey, excuse me, have you seen my food? I put it on the table. There was some pizza and some fries. I just went to go get my juice and I came back and now it's gone."

For the record, I never wanted confrontation. I didn't want to fight. I didn't want to argue. I just wanted to be left alone.

Suddenly, a kid came up behind me and said, "I know where it is."

I turned around and got excited.

"Yeah, I know where it is," he said again. "It's in the garbage."

"It's in the garbage? Why?"

"Because I put it there."

I walked over to the garbage can and looked inside. Lo and behold, there was a perfectly fine slice of pizza and fries.

I walked over to him. "Why did you throw my food in the garbage?"

"Because I know you're not going to do anything about it."

I started to walk away, noticing all eyes were on me. He kept on gloating about how he threw my food away, and how I wasn't going to do anything about it. Then he stood up and trailed me, taking it to another level.

I felt like maybe I could still get out of this situation without getting into a fight, and that's when he pushed me. My mother and father always told me: "If somebody hits you, you better hit them back, especially if you've already had a situation where you told people that this is what you're dealing with."

Now, mind you, before I confronted my peers about my food, I asked the teachers beforehand if they saw anything and they said they hadn't or whatever. I had to assume they weren't going to do anything about the situation. Not to mention, this kid had been picking on me for a while.

When he pushed me again, I spun around and kicked him in the nose and broke it. It was bleeding all over the place and the next thing I knew, I was sitting in the principal's office.

"Well, Brad, you didn't have to do that."

"I've been complaining to you guys for I don't know how long about this kid bothering me and picking on me, making fun of my height and touching my hair, hitting me, making fun of my skin changing colors because I'm light-skinned and you know we bruise easily. He's called me all kinds of names like shrimp fried rice, midget, and shorty, and now you want to get mad at me because I finally kicked this kid in the face for throwing all my food in the garbage?!"

"Calm down," the principal said. "We can get you some more food. You didn't have to break his nose."

"I didn't know that was going to happen. That's the first time I've ever kicked anybody in the face."

Needless to say, that was the very last fight that I got into with that kid. I got into a couple other rumbles here and there, but nothing serious. By that point, people recognized that I wasn't afraid to fight anymore. I wasn't going to let anyone beat me up for the sake of picking on me. You were going to have to beat me in a fight. If you wanted a W, you were going to have to earn it.

The school called my parents and told them all about the incident in the cafeteria. When I got home, my mom asked, "Is this the same boy who's been bothering you?"

I said, "Yeah, it's been going on for a while."

"Okay, well, I understand. Hopefully this will be the last time it happens."

My dad only had one question: "Did you win?"

"Well, Dad, he has a broken nose and I think I'm good."

"Well, goddammit, there we go."

And that was the end of that conversation.

Like my father had explained to me before, if somebody bothers me for a long period of time and they put their hands on me—"You're going to have to fight back. Otherwise, every single day somebody is going to be picking on you or trying to beat you up."

In retrospect, violence shouldn't have been the go-to solution for that incident. There's more than enough violence to go around and, at some point, someone has to be strong enough, big enough, and brave enough try a different approach. I should've been that guy. I think we need to be better as a society and respect that, despite our differences and our backgrounds, we're all human. We all just want to be understood and accepted—that's it. We all want someone to validate us and ease our strife. I believe this kid picked on me for so long because he had issues of his own to deal with, as did I. It doesn't excuse his bullying, and it doesn't excuse my aggression. But my particular upbringing showed me that in order to survive and handle my business, oftentimes, a fist to the face was necessary. Violence ruled my home, my community, and my mentality. I didn't know any other way. It was feast or famine. Kill or be killed. And nobody wanted to fall prey to anyone else, so we all did what we thought we had to in order to survive the day—or survive lunch as a middle schooler.

CHAPTER 7
A Whole New World

When I was a little older, my parents decided that it would be best for me to move with my father to the suburb of East Windsor, New Jersey. I was completely against this because I didn't want to leave my mother, my grandmother, my sister, and the rest of my family and friends. My mom said that she couldn't teach me how to become a man, only a man could teach a boy how to become a man, so I had to live with my father and paternal grandparents in East Windsor—my father was staying in their home.

When I first arrived, it was a huge culture shock. Where were all the bright lights and loud noises of the city? There were no sirens or police cars flying down the streets. No gunshots in the middle of the night. My sister and I have had to run from the sound of gunshots before, that was nothing new. Moving to the 'burbs, however, I couldn't hear a thing after dark…just crickets. Now *that* scared me. It was so quiet. The first couple of days, it was hard for me to fall asleep because I was used to the sounds of the city.

The sky was so clear that I could see the constellations they would teach us about in school. My father had a hard time adjusting to the area as well. It was so bad for him that he would drive all the way back to Jersey City just to hear the sounds of the city.

To top it off, I'd never really been around Caucasian people before. I'd only known one, really, and that was an old friend I had back in kindergarten—Giorgio Belloni.

Living with my dad's parents was a completely different experience altogether. Charles and Bette Butler weren't just God-fearing, they actually went to church every week. They never cursed, yelled, or argued. Dad and I were expected to live by their rules, and that's all there was to it. You didn't really get a say in anything if you were a child. I love them both to death, but they had a different way of raising children than Mom, Dad, and Grandma Brenda. And they were Seventh-day Adventists, meaning they believed in keeping the Sabbath holy, which meant we went to church on Saturdays. After sundown on a Friday, there was no playing outside, no work, and no spending money of any sort. No TV, no toys, no comic books, and no video games. I felt like I was in jail. If my grandparents thought they were going to get my dad and me to follow the rules and go to church every Saturday, they must've been crazy. The only time my dad agreed to go was when my grandfather's friend, Rudy Snelling, would make a special visit to sing for the congregation.

Rudy had that old soulful voice and knew how to belt out those notes. My grandfather and Rudy had been good friends for a long time, so he would invite Rudy to come sing once a year. My grandfather would make a huge deal out of it and call our entire family and ask them to come and listen. It was hilarious because I got to watch all my aunts and uncles on my dad's side of the family sit through what I had to deal with every Saturday. Most of them nodded off and tried to sneak out.

Our church was small and rundown, paint chipping off the sides, old wood, leaky roof…. The building was located right in Hightstown, near Main Street. I could count all the members on both hands. I didn't have a problem with going to church in the past, but I was pissed about spending six hours there on a Saturday evening when I wanted to play outside and watch cartoons after a long week of school. I remember one day when I'd gotten a little older, I couldn't take it anymore. I said, "Dad, I can't keep going back to that church. I can't stand it there. I don't have a problem with church, I just don't like that one."

"All right," he said. "I know it's kind of rough. I'll talk to your grandparents."

I almost did a backflip—I'd finally gotten my Saturdays back.

I remember my first day of school. I was at Ethel McKnight. It was right across the street from my house on Edison Drive. I remember the first day, for whatever reason, my dad picked out my clothes for me. I had blue jeans and a Polo on. My dad thought it would be a good idea for me to wear these red boots, all red, triple red. I couldn't stand them, but my dad said he thought they looked nice, so I wore them. I remember walking to school and I didn't think it was a big deal, so I just crossed the street. There weren't any cars around, so I walked across the street and then I can hear this lady from way down the streets saying, "Hey, what are you doing? You can't just walk across the street." I'm like, "Lady, what are you talking about? I'm going to school."

She said, "Come on down here."

I walked over there and she said, "I'm the crossing guard. You have to cross the street where I'm at so we can make sure you get across safely."

Blew my mind.

"Are you serious? You want me to walk to where you're at just to cross the damn street? Lady, I know how to cross the street."

That's how different things were in the 'burbs. I said, "All right," then turned and walked toward the school.

As I was leaving, the lady yelled, "Hey, kid."

I turned back around. "Yes, ma'am?"

"Nice shoes."

"Thank you," I said, and continued my walk.

When I first looked at the school, it was a weird shape. It had a big dome on top of it. It's just the weirdest shape I've ever seen for a school. Now, it doesn't look like that. They reconstructed the whole thing, but it was unique and that's how it stood out.

I remember going inside and lining up with all the other kids. I was one of the only black kids, whereas with every other school I'd attended, there were a bunch of black kids. I was standing there, just looking at everybody else, thinking to myself, *I look so much different compared to them.* Braids in my hair, Polo T-shirt on my back, blue jeans, red boots…. The other boys had khaki shorts on with bright-colored sneakers. They all had the same hairstyle, too—gelled and flipped up in the front like a tidal wave.

I was thinking, *Umm, okay, so I guess you want to look like everyone else, huh?*

The kid standing next to me said, "Hey, what's up?"

As it turns out, his name was Brandon.

I said, "Hey, Brandon. My name is Brad."

"Oh, wow, that's cool," he said. "You new?"

"Yeah."

He was standing there with a Walkman, headphones slung around his neck. He said, "Hey, have you heard the new Backstreet Boys album?"

"Blackstreet? Yeah, I like Blackstreet."

"No, no, no, not Blackstreet, Backstreet Boys."

"Yeah, that's what I said, Blackstreet. I don't know what a Backstreet Boy is. You mean Blackstreet?"

"No, no, no. Here, just listen."

He took his headphones off and placed them over my ears. Then he hit play.

"What is this, bro? This is not what I thought it was."

"Yeah, these are the Backstreet Boys. I don't know what Blackstreet is," he said.

We're definitely not in Kansas anymore.

"Things are just so different here. How am I ever supposed to get used to this? The music is not the same. People don't dress the same. Their hairstyles aren't the same. Our skin colors aren't the same. The culture is completely different. Man, it doesn't even sound the same out here. I don't see any black girls, either. Who am I supposed to talk to?"

"Me," he offered.

And just like that, I made my first new friend.

Within the first two weeks of attending a new school, they put me in special ed classes. I remember the teacher saying, "Hey, guys, we're going to have a spelling bee, so I'm going to walk around and hand out the form. If you want to be in it, sign your name."

She walked around the tables and passed out flyers to all the kids who had their hand raised. I raised mine and she waved me off. That was the first time in school where I truly felt like I wasn't smart enough. Why couldn't I have one? Why couldn't I try?

I sat with my head down for the rest of the class.

CHAPTER 8
I'm Not Special

Soon after the spelling bee incident, I had a meeting with my mom and the child study team. They told me they were going to place me in special ed classes to help me catch up. Now, I'm no rocket scientist, but even at eight years old, I knew that it was going to be impossible for me to catch up if everyone was moving at a faster pace.

I remember sitting at the table, crying, begging them not to put me in special ed classes. I'd never seen the special ed class, but I'd heard stories and didn't want to be a part of it. I wasn't the most book smart, but I was a solid C student. I did have to take summer school once or twice, but I never would have imagined that I'd get thrown in special ed classes. I begged my mom. I begged the counselors. I told them that I'd do whatever they wanted me to do.

"Mom, I'll clean my room. I'll take out the garbage. I'll do extra chores. I'll work harder, I promise. I'll do whatever you want me to do, but, please, don't let them put me in these classes. I don't want to be considered a special ed kid. I'm not a special ed kid. I'm not special."

One of the ladies from the child study team said, "But, Brad, do you know what the word special means?"

"Yeah. I know what the word special means, but I don't think that's what you mean when you're talking about me."

She said, "Well, listen, this is a dictionary, and we're going to look at the word special and I'm going to read to you the definition."

How insulting.

I said, "I hear you, but none of this sounds or feels right."

I ended up in special ed. Classes were much smaller. I had the same teachers over and over again, and there were actually some kids in those classes that really needed to be in special ed because they had a learning disability. I didn't feel like I had a learning disability. I just felt like I learned differently from other people. Some people can retain information from just reading. I wasn't that guy. I needed hands-on experience.

If you want me to understand the value of money, then you need to explain how money's going to affect my daily life. Show me how to balance a checkbook. Don't just say, "It's important to save money." You need to tell me why. Why do I need to save money? And how do I go about accomplishing that? Because, for me, I never could understand the examples they tried to teach me in school. I never really liked those problem-solving questions they'd give you in math class: *Well, Johnny has ten Snicker bars, and Johnny has eaten eight of those. What does Johnny now have?* I would be the kid who'd raise my hand and say, "Johnny has diabetes." Then I'd get kicked out of class.

I struggled with the idea of being in those classes because I always felt like I was smarter than what everyone made me out to be. It also didn't help that Grandma Brenda would always tell me that I was a genius. *Sure, Grandma, your grandson in special ed is a genius. Thanks for the pep talk.*

As you can probably imagine, I got into a lot of fights due to my frustration and embarrassment. I not only felt embarrassed for myself, I felt embarrassed on behalf of my family. *They didn't put Mom in special ed classes. They didn't put Dad in special ed classes. Ciji wasn't in special ed, so why am I?*

I ended up being stuck in those classes all the way through high school, and I spent years hiding it from my friends and family. I didn't allow girls to get close. I avoided getting in relationships because I knew, at some point, I was going to have to tell them that I was in special ed—that I wasn't smart, and I wasn't special.

There were some funny moments throughout the journey, though. I once watched a kid, who was so high on PCP that he could give Jesus Christ a high five, stop our entire class in the middle of a midterm exam to tell everyone that he knows karate and was about to show us. If only you could have seen the look on our teacher's face. The first thought that went through my head was, *Oh, please, God, don't tempt me with a good time. You know I live for these moments.*

When I saw him position himself in the karate kid stance, I said, "Oh, this is not a drill."

Being the great classmate that I am, I didn't want to get in the way of his performance, so I made sure to slide my desk back and give him all the room he needed. Our teacher told everyone to ignore him, that he was seeking attention. After all the years of living in Jersey City and seeing how athletic crack heads could be, I knew exactly what high and crazy looked like. This was home. I also knew what type of superhuman feats high people were capable of, so there was no way I was about to miss this.

Most of the kids went back to work, but the ones like me who knew better put their pencils down, kept their head up, and their eyes wide open. I just knew he was about to do some crazy shit, and boy he didn't disappoint. Those drugs must have kicked into overdrive because after he set up his flying crane stance, he yelled, "WHHHHOOOAAAA," took two good steps like an Olympic long jumper, soared through the air, and did a Bruce Lee flying dragon kick. It was like I watched the whole thing play out in slow motion. This kid had zero to no hang time, and he didn't brace himself for impact. He landed on three desks, breaking two of them in half. He laid on the ground for no longer five seconds before the drugs kicked in again and he was back on his feet.

By this point, the party was over. Our teacher had already called for security. When they arrived, they dragged the kid out of the classroom. He was expelled, so I never saw him again after that.

The worst thing I ever dealt with in special ed was when the administrators changed the curriculum for our reading classes in middle school. Normally, we would get different books that we read at home or in class, then we talked about it or took a test on it. Not this semester. The moment we all set foot in the classroom, we could tell something was different. Our teacher, Mrs. D, didn't even bother to tell students to quiet down, stop the horseplay, or have a seat. She just sat at her desk with a blank look on her face.

When we started to pick up the vibe, everybody sat down and waited for instructions. Now, you know something is wrong when every kid in a special ed class is sitting still, waiting to hear instructions.

She said, "Okay, there have been some changes, this semester we will be doing our classwork a bit differently."

She walked around the room, handing out reading workbooks, and told us not to open them.

"I'm going to go over the instructions with you. Put your name on the top of the booklet and open to page one. I will read the first sentence on the page, and when I give the command, you will repeat that sentence out loud."

I raised my hand. "Ahh…. Mrs. D, you know we can read on our own, right?"

"Brad, please let me teach."

I thought to myself, *Okay, maybe she is right. Maybe this is a new way to help us build on our reading skills.* Then she started to read from the book.

"Dave plays with his red ball."

CLICK!

Okay…. What the hell was that?

No one spoke the first time, so she tried it again.

"Dave plays with his red ball."

CLICK!

Still, no one spoke.

"Listen, this is what we have to do in this class, and if you want to pass, you need to follow the instructions," Mrs. D said.

I knew something was wrong. I could just tell by the tone of her voice that she was just as disgusted to be teaching the lesson this way as we were to have to participate in it.

She read the sentence a third time. This time, the class repeated the sentence after the click. I looked around the room with my jaw to the floor, in disbelief. My mother and father have always told me you have to stand for what you believe in, and I know I was in special ed classes, but I was no one's fool. I refused to allow myself to feel belittled in an environment that I was supposed to consider a place to learn and feel comfortable doing so.

After a while, Mrs. D noticed that I wasn't reading.

She stopped and said, "Brad, why aren't you reading like everyone else?"

"Because I'm not a dog. That is a is a clicker used to train dogs, and you know my reading level is way higher than this."

"Brad, please read along with us. I know this is easy for most of you, and I know you're not a dog, it's just a tool they want us to use."

"All due respect, I'm not doing it, Mrs. D. I'm not stupid. I can read."

"Well, if you're not going to cooperate, I'm going to have to send to you to the principal's office. So, what's it gonna be? You stay here with us and read, or you have to leave."

"Write me a pass, please."

"Brad, you can stay in the class if you just participate like everyone else."

"I'd like to go to the principal's office, please."

I'd never felt so exploited before in a classroom. Mrs. D was always big on pushing us to work harder, to do the best we could. That's why she had a hard time making eye contact with us that day. She knew teaching those lessons went against everything she believed in. She was known for being a tough lady, but she always wanted the best for her students. Always. Something tells me that when no one was looking, she shed some tears that day.

I went down to the principal's office and sat in the chair.

"Brad, what are you doing in my office? What did you do now?"

I told the principal about the situation. He said he understood my side of the story, but I'd still have to go back to class and do the work. I told him wasn't going to do it because I felt it was an insult to my reading ability and dehumanizing as a whole.

He said, "Brad, I think you're a good kid, and I don't want you to get in trouble, but if you don't go back to class, I'm going to have to call your mother."

I started rattling off her work number.

"What are you doing?" the principal asked.

"I'm giving you her work number."

After they talked to my mom, I still had to do the work in the booklet, however, they left me alone when it came to reading out loud. Eventually, Mrs. D got rid of the clicker anyway—a win for everyone.

CHAPTER 9
Deuce

One of the reasons I was having such a difficult time adjusting to this new school was because I felt there was no one I could really relate to. I'd managed to make a few new friends here and there, but it wasn't the same as back home. Thankfully, little did I know, the tides were about to turn.

One afternoon, I was outside playing Pokémon with some of my friends from the neighborhood when a U-Haul pulled in to one of the driveways on our street. Sitting on the passenger side was a kid who looked a lot like me—African American.

He hopped out of the truck and helped his family move all the boxes into the house. My friends and I all got up to see who these people were.

The boy came back out and said, "Hey, what are you guys doing?"

"We're just playing Pokémon cards. You new around here? You guys moving in?"

"Yeah."

"What's up? My name is Brad." I reached out and shook his hand.

"Hey, what's up? My name is Sam."

That was the start of a lifelong friendship. Brad Butler and Sam Salter would eventually go on to become brothers, not just friends. God knew the best thing He could do for us was to allow our paths to cross.

I tried doing things as best as I could. It was my way of trying to make up for being in special ed classes. Sports was one of the only outlets I had aside from art. I always had an eye for art and a natural drawing talent. My grandmother could draw really well, so she taught me how to draw and to work on my skills.

The great thing about having Sam around was I had somebody that could rival me in every sport. Whereas before, I was the best athlete on the block. Nobody could touch me. I would burn anybody in a race. What? Basketball! I wasn't even a basketball player, but I knew I was going to shoot the lights out on anybody from that neighborhood. Hockey! You know damn well we don't play hockey, but guess what? Street hockey, I was going to win. Football, don't even get me started. They didn't stand a chance. If I was on the team, we were winning.

Now, all of a sudden, this new guy shows up, dark skin, tall dude, super athletic with a crazy build that I hadn't seen for a kid my size and my age. Let me tell you, my boy Sam, fast as the lightning. It was the same thing whenever we would race—his legs were much longer. I would beat him for about half the race and then his stride would kick in. I didn't actually beat Sam in a race until my junior year in high school. Every sport we played turned into a competition. Everything we did turned into a competition and that was part of the reason why we became such great friends.

On top of that, his family welcomed me with open arms. Ms. Walker, Sam's mom, became a second mother to me. Sam was actually the first person who introduced me to playing football on a team. I owe every award and piece of success I have to him because if it weren't for him pushing me to play, maybe I never would have touched the field. He was there for some of my best and worst moments. The first touchdown I ever made came from Sam diving in the way to block two defenders as I sprinted to a 99-yard kick return to the crib. He was also there the day I wanted to give up playing football after I'd had the worst flag football game of my life. I think I gave up 3 or 4 touchdowns and got hit with every route on the wide receiver route tree. Sam was right there to tell me I'd just had a bad day, and he knew what I was capable of, so he wasn't going to allow me to quit.

I used to play out in the streets and that was cool, but when Sam and his cousins said, "Hey, why don't we play for Hightstown Pop Warner team?" I thought to myself, *That would be a great idea. There's no way we're going to lose.*

Unfortunately, that little dream was short-lived because Sam's cousins didn't end up playing. Instead, they moved to Trenton, so that just left Sam and me. Still, I thought he and I could do this.

I went home and asked my father.

"Hey, Dad, I think I want to play football."

He said, "Are you serious? You really want to play football? You've never really shown interest in football. I know you play it every now and then outside, but you've never said anything about wanting to play for a real team."

"Yeah, I know, but Sam and I went down to check it out and I think it would be a good idea. Like, why not?"

He contemplated. "Well, listen, I don't have a problem with you playing football. That's cool, but how much does it cost?"

"One hundred dollars and that's for everything."

"Okay," he replied. "But I'm telling you this right now. If I pay this money for you to play football, you are going to finish the season. There's no quitting."

"No, Dad, I'm cool. I never quit anything," I reminded him.

"Yeah, you're right, but I'm just letting you know I'm making an investment."

"Yeah, I know, I know. Come on, Dad, please. I really want to play. Sam and I are both going to play together."

"Fine, all right. I know you and Sam are attached at the hip, so okay."

That was the start of me playing football.

I went out for the team and I distinctly remember us waiting in line to weigh in. The money had been paid. Everything was ready to go. They weighed Sam and everybody else. Then it was my turn to step on the scale.

"Oh, you're not going to be able to play," the guy said.

"What do you mean? Why? My dad paid his money like everybody else. Why can't I play? I'm fast, you need me."

He said, "Well, it's not about your speed or the money. You're under the weight limit."

"I'm under the weight limit?" I asked.

"Yes."

"How much do I have to weigh?"

"At least one hundred pounds."

"Okay…. How much do I weigh?"

"Eighty-five," he replied.

"I could just go eat some more. I can put the weight on. I mean, it's not really that big of a thing. What's the problem with me not being one hundred pounds?"

"Well, we're worried about you getting hurt," he explained.

"I wouldn't blame you guys if I got hurt. I'm not going to get hurt anyway. I've been playing sports for I don't know how many years."

"Yeah, but not on this level with pads and stuff."

"What are you saying?"

He said, "You can be on the team, but you can't actually play in any of the games unless you make weight before the game. We'll have to weigh you before every single one. If you're not one hundred pounds, you won't be able to play."

"So, I still have time?"

"Yeah, you can practice and train, but when it's game time, you have to weigh at least one hundred pounds."

"Okay. I can do that."

I went home later that day and told my dad. He said, "You're going to have to start eating more."

No kidding. And I did. I would weigh myself every day. I was able to get myself up to about ninety pounds, but I definitely didn't hit the full hundred. I wanted to play so badly that I would go out onto the field before weigh-in and find rocks, then stuff them in my pockets and throw sweatpants on over my shorts so that my coaches couldn't see.

Sometimes I'd weigh myself and I'd be around 105. I think at one time I actually put too many rocks in by accident and I was roughly 110 pounds. My coaches were like, "Great job, Brad. You're really putting on some weight." I was just determined to play. And I didn't like people telling me what I could and couldn't do.

Now, in regard to Pop Warner, I really didn't get to play as much as I'd liked on offense. They played me on defense. I had a good experience learning my very first year how to play football, and that's when I realized I had a deep love for the game. It was funny; the first number I was given was 24. I brought the jersey home and showed it to my father.

"Hey, Dad, they gave me number 24."

"Seriously? That was my number."

"I know. How cool is that?"

The following day we had a snow day, so everyone wanted to go out and play football in the snow. Everyone but Sam. We all talked him into playing. We were having a good time, and on the last drive of the game, someone landed on Sam's leg the wrong way. Sam knew immediately something was wrong, so some of the kids playing helped carry him home. I had to leave after the game because I had to take a shower and change my clothes for work.

When I got off work, I went to check on him. Sam's family told me he was in the hospital.

"Did he pull a muscle or break it?" I asked.

They said he had a blood clot that traveled up his leg and almost made it to his heart, but they were able to perform emergency surgery to release the pressure. I was the only friend that would go with Sam's mom early in the morning before school to go see him. It was tough to see my brother in so much pain. He had to spend almost his entire junior year in the hospital and at home. Thankfully, my brother is tough. He made a full recovery only to finish playing football for his senior year, but he never got the chance to play in college because he dealt with high blood pressure as a result of the injury. I knew how much playing football meant to him, I knew how much not playing hurt him. If anyone had a shot at playing for a college team, it was Sam. I never told Sam this, but the only reason I played for as long as I did was to go as far as I could for him. I didn't want to take the opportunity for granted when I knew Sam would kill to be in the game. So, Sam, every championship, every award, every stat I've ever achieved was for you, bro. Without your support, none of it would've been possible.

Thanks, **Deuce #22**

CHAPTER 10
Uphill Battle

High school was cool. I don't really have too many bad memories. To me, I kind of just looked at it as I go to school, I do my work, I play sports, I go home. As long as I maintained a C average, I could continue to play sports. Normally, my best grades came during football season because I knew I had to keep my grades up. But I was still stuck in the special ed classes, still avoiding people because I didn't want them to know.

Later on in my high school career, I started doing more research on special ed classes and actually found a teacher who didn't mind telling me all the information that I really needed to know. She told me, "Listen, if you work hard, you can possibly get out of special ed classes."

I started working harder, getting As and Bs, trying to prove to them that, *hey, you may have put me in the special ed class, but you guys got it wrong. I really don't need to be in here.* I don't know if you've ever seen the movie *Roman J. Israel, Esq.*, but Denzel Washington plays a lawyer who has devoted his life to his career, and by doing so, he doesn't have much of a social life and is kind of disconnected from the world. Now, I'm not saying my story is exactly like his, but there is one part in the movie where he's having a bad day and he ends up getting robbed. While he's getting beat up, trying to protect himself from the punches, he keeps yelling at the robber, "You've got the wrong guy! You've got the wrong guy!"

For whatever reason, I couldn't help but feel like that was me. Every day, trapped in those classes, smiling on the outside but screaming on the inside, crying, "*Let me out! You've got the guy, you've got the wrong guy. I'm not stupid, I'm not special. Why won't anyone listen to me? Why won't anyone help me?*"

It became hard for me to ask for help and express my feelings because I'd gotten so used to feeling like no one took me seriously, or that no one even cared. I would know I needed help with something, but I wouldn't ask because I feared people would look down on me and call me stupid. I know kids call each other stupid, dumb, retarded all the time, but I feel like if you're in special ed classes, you really take those words to heart.

I've heard many arguments between students in those classes, but it was rare for us to call one other dumb, stupid, or retarded. Those words cut too deep, especially the word retarded. I've seen some of the nicest and shyest kids go from 0–60 after someone called them retarded. I've always been pretty good at keeping my cool on the outside when someone would call me that, mostly because I knew if I got mad enough, I would punch them. And violence was a no-go at this point in my life. I was maturing.

After enough hard work and dedication, the school finally placed me in a mainstream geometry class, and I did well. I understood the problems and took it all seriously. After the term was over, I said, "Hey, do you guys think I might be able to get out of the special ed classes? I did well in this class."

They said they'd look into it, but nothing ever happened.

At this point, I kind of just gave up. My thought process was, *Why am I going to put forth all my effort to try and get out of the special ed classes when it's not going to help?* I lost my fight to maintain the best grades possible. I started blowing things off. I stopped putting up forth my best effort. I talked to one of my teachers, one who helped me out a lot. Her name was Mrs. Inglisa. She said, "Brad,

I can't tell you exactly how special ed classes work. The only thing I can tell you is that if you work hard, you can get out of these classes. You really are gifted. You have to use your gift."

Just then, something clicked. *She said the word gifted.* Normally people would say I was special, and I couldn't stand it because I felt like it was connected to the classes I was stuck in. Then she continued, "But I'd also like you to do your research. Find out whatever it is that you can find out about the classes and how to get to the next level if you have any aspirations of going to college."

"Okay," I said. So that's what I did.

By that time we had the Internet, so I could just look up whatever information I wanted. Either that or I could ask around school and talk to other people. Thankfully, with some thorough research, I found out that I wasn't actually getting college credits. That meant if I did decide to go to a college, I'd have to start with 101 classes, which would probably set me back a full year.

Then I found out a close friend of mine, who was a great athlete and had a bunch of scholarships, had all his scholarships taken away because he was in special ed classes and they didn't tell him he wasn't getting college credits. They just let him go. They let him go through the system. They let him continue to be a great athlete, but never once did they tell him that being in those classes was going to stop him from being able to go to the colleges that were sending him scholarships. That's probably one of the most heartbreaking things I've ever heard. From that point on, I said, "I'm definitely going to college. I'm going to find a way to make it happen."

I had one of the counselors in the IEP meeting ask me what I wanted to do with my life. What did I want to do next? They offered me the opportunity to go to Vo-tech—a vocational-technical school—because they knew I was good at art. They said, "Brad, why don't you try going into the trade school. Vo-tech would be good for you."

I said, "Well, I'm thinking about going to college."

"We're not sure if that would be the best option for you."

I said, "Why not?"

"Well, you haven't really had that type of training, you haven't learned enough where you would be able to handle a college curriculum."

The biggest mistake anyone can make is telling me I can't do something. After that moment, I made it my personal mission to go to college. My mother's words came floating back: "*Hey, Brad, I know you're in special ed classes, but if you want to go to college, you can go. Don't let anyone tell you that you can't if that's what you want to do.*"

While I was going through my middle school and high school years, my mom went off to the school and got her bachelor's, and then she got her master's degree. She showed me the blueprint that it could be done, that I could go off to school and be successful at the college level. Why? Because I felt like it was in my gene pool. My mom was able to do it, so I should be able to do it too, right?

The decision was made. I was going to find a way to go to college, and I was going to find a way to be successful. Then my father ended up having a brain aneurysm due to stress at his job. He was in a medically-induced coma for about three months. During this time, my mother, my sister, and both sides of the family started to plan for the worst, just in case my father didn't make it. My mother said, "If we're going to do this and we're going to fight to try to keep your father alive and give him a second chance, then we're going to give him the best medical care possible."

We sent my father to Kessler Hospital. It's the same hospital they put Christopher Reeve in, the guy who played Superman. Translation: it's a serious facility, and it cost some serious money. It put our family in six-figure debt, maxing out all credit cards, loans, anything we could use to help my father. It was crazy seeing my father connected to all those machines, tubes coming out of his mouth and nose to drain all the blood. Thankfully, my father ended up having a full recovery. During this time, I was still going to school and held down a part-time job at ShopRite.

I also had a girlfriend who I'd been with since sophomore year, and everything was cool before my dad got sick. I saved my money to take my girl to the movies and out to eat on Friday nights. But things changed. My father was the breadwinner and the man of the house. With him being in a coma for three months, that left me with a responsibility of being the man of the house. ShopRite money was now used to buy groceries for my grandparents instead of taking my girlfriend out. Life was different. I didn't tell any of my friends besides Sam and my girlfriend. I didn't tell any of the staff at the school because I didn't know what was going to happen to my father, but I always believed that he was going to have a full recovery.

We never know what the future holds, but I just never had that sinking feeling that we were going to lose him. I fully believed that I would still have my father in my life. I remember one day, the principal came to one of my classes and pulled me out while I was taking a test and said, "Hey, Brad, how are you doing?"

"I'm fine. What did I do?"

He said, "Oh, no, no. You didn't do anything. We just talked to your mother and we understand that your father had a brain aneurysm. Why didn't you tell us?"

I said, "No disrespect, but how was telling you going to help?"

"Well, we could have offered you extra time to take a test and things like that."

"Offering me extra time to take a test isn't going to help me get through the situation. My family is in six-figure debt. Unless you guys were going to offer us some money, I don't see how you guys were going to be able to help us."

"I understand. If there's anything we can do to help, please let us know."

Thankfully, God allowed my father to have a full recovery walking, talking, reading, writing, doing anything that a normal able-bodied male can do. However, when he came home, there were still some adjustments that needed to be made. I had to read his mail for him until his memory came back and he was able to read again. I had to help handle the finances. I had to help out a lot more with my grandparents and make sure they had everything they needed.

CHAPTER 11

Bend Don't Break

Over time, things got better because my dad was able to handle more and more each day. After I graduated from Hightstown High, I decided that summer I was going to go right to college. Thank God my grandparents on my dad's side gave me their car—they weren't able to drive anymore. It was a 2003 gold Buick Century. Wide body, smoothest ride ever. All my friends wanted to ride in my car because it had so much space, but I was so focused on trying to do well in school I didn't want to go out much. I made a decision to go to Mercer County Community College that summer. I joined the EOF program and they enrolled me in summer classes. I didn't have to worry about paying for tuition in the summer as an EOF student as long as I passed my classes with a C or better.

I remember my very first class. It was a transitioning to college class. My professor gave me my first essay. I'd never written one before. Being in special

73

ed classes, we didn't do that, so the pressure was on. I didn't know anything about MLA and APA format, or the proper way to break down an essay and make sure you don't have grammatical errors.

The essay had to be three pages. I wrote my paper and handed it in with confidence, but I'd lost track of time because I handed it in a day late. I thought, *Handing in a paper a day late, I mean, I still can get a good grade. I don't think she's going to take points off. They didn't take points off when I was in high school and I was in special ed classes. I don't think it's going to be much different, right?* Wrong.

The professor handed it back and informed me that I was not a very good writer and that I needed a whole lot of work if I intended to be successful in college. She let me know that the first issue was that I handed in my paper a day late. She was dropping my grade an entire letter grade. I said, "Okay. Well, that just means I'm not going to get an A. I can still get a B though, right?"

She started grading it and I ended up with a D. She suggested I get a tutor if I wanted to have a chance at passing the class.

I quickly realized that college and special ed were completely different. Heck, college was different from mainstream classes. If I was going to be successful, no one else was going to help me with this. No one else was going to be able to write these papers for me. It was time to seek the help I needed. I was going to have to get tutors. I was going to have to work way harder, stay up later, and read more in order for this to work. And that's exactly what I did. I worked harder. I read more. I wrote more. I had to rewrite some papers to get it right. I did whatever I had to do, and I got through the semester. I was really happy because I was able to do it all on my own.

I finished my summer classes and attempted to sign up for fall semester. I went to go see my counselor, whose name was Mr. Al-Lateef Farmer. He said, "Good job passing summer classes. Have you decided on a major?"

I decided to pursue a degree in fine arts. I signed up for fall classes and as he was trying to process it, he said, "Wait a minute. Brad, it's saying that you don't have funding. You filled out your FAFSA form, right?"

"What's a FAFSA?" I asked.

"Oh my God. You didn't fill out the FAFSA forms?"

"No, I don't even know what a FAFSA is."

He said, "Well, Brad, you have to pay for school unless you're paying for it with cash."

"Cash? I don't have any money. I'm broke. You know I'm broke, I told you that before I got here."

"Well, then you need FAFSA."

"Okay…. Where's the form at and I'll go fill it out."

"Brad, the FAFSA forms needed to be filled out weeks ago."

"What does that mean? I can't fill it out now?"

"No, we can fill it out now. We can fill out the forms but, Brad, I don't know if you're going to have the money to cover full semester. You might end up getting dropped from classes."

I was like, "Wait a minute. You're telling me I just worked my butt off this whole summer to pass those classes so I could be able to take these classes in the fall, and now you're saying it's a strong possibility that may not even happen because I forgot to fill some forms out? Forms I didn't even know about?"

"Yes, Brad."

My eyes started to water. I felt so stupid, like I'd worked so hard. How did I miss that? Obviously, the schooling had to be paid for and I hadn't made any payments.

I sat in the chair with my head down, feeling utterly defeated by the situation. I remember a tear falling from my eyes and landing on my pants.

"Don't worry, Brad. We're going to figure this out," Mr. Farmer said. "You're a good kid and you did everything you could. You didn't know. We're going to get you in those classes. We're going to find a way to get this taken care of."

The only thing I could think of in the back of my mind was, *Yeah, okay, if you say so. To me, it sounds like it's a done deal. How am I going to explain this to Mom and Dad?* I told my mom I was going to go to college—I promised her—and now I had to turn around and tell her that I wasn't going to be able to go after all. Great. Here I go, shaming the family again.

Thank God for the EOF program and Mercer County Community College and all the counselors like Mr. Farmer, because without them, I don't think there's any way I would have made it through. I overcame that situation and they helped me get some emergency FAFSA money to be able to pay for my tuition and my books. I told them I'd do whatever they wanted me to. I'd take whatever classes they wanted me to take. All because they worked their butts off and went above and beyond to help me. I can count on one hand how many people have done that for me in my lifetime. They legitimately wanted the best for me.

I made it through the program and graduated from Mercer County Community College. The funny thing about it is, a lot of the friends I made from Ewing,

Trenton, Princeton, West Windsor…they were all surprised that I graduated. They didn't think I was smart enough or capable enough to do it.

In the graduating class, there was a summer group that we had that I came in with. It consisted of about seventy kids. From that group, only two people ended up graduating from the 2006 EOF summer class—me and a girl whose name I don't remember, unfortunately.

I may have graduated, but everything I had to go through to get my associate's degree really tested my commitment and faith. While struggling to get my degree, dealing with financial hardships, and learning how to be the man of the house, I suffered my first real heartbreak. My high school sweetheart broke my heart when she ended our four-year relationship. She was never able to give me a real reason why, so I just left it as we grew apart and she wanted to see other people. I understood, but it didn't make it hurt any less. My mother told me that if there was any pain in the world that she wished she could take away for me, it would be my first heartbreak. She said it's a pain unlike anything you've ever felt. She was right. I felt so much pain that it started to make me physically ill. Some days, I thought it'd never end. I couldn't sleep, eat, or even think straight. I remember my father and I went to Wendy's to pick up some food for my grandparents. We were sitting in the drive-thru, waiting to get our food. My dad turned to me and said, "Listen, son, I know you're still mad about the break-up with your ex, but you gotta snap out of it."

It's crazy how much power a father has when he speaks to his son. My mom let me know she was there for me any time I needed to talk. My sister let me know that my ex was probably out running the streets having a good old time not thinking about me so I'd better get my mind right, but my father made me realize that I was a man now, and I couldn't let her or anything else get in the way of my responsibilities. After that it seemed like out of nowhere, each day got better and better. I learned to smile again and remembered what it felt like to be happy.

After I got past the heartbreak, I started talking to more people, networking, getting back to being myself. What really helped was when we started a football club on campus. Everybody would come out to watch us play football in the quad. We loved the attention. Playing football at Mercer was how a met a lot of my good friends from Trenton, like Ant Live, Yuk, JK, Base Head, Ash, Chop, J. Dot, Smooth, JJ, Baby Mike, Stu, Rugby, McLovin', Chavis, and many more. All of our street football games were recorded by our friend, Booth. We still have all the videos on YouTube under "Mercer Football." Check it out if you ever want to see some good, old-fashioned street football.

After a while we took the best players that we had from MCCC and we formed a team called Riot Squad, and later B.I.C.—a team owned by another good friend, CaBootz. We played in a league called Town Beef, which is now known as A7FL. I truly made some lifelong friends at MCCC, and the city of Trenton has shown me nothing but love over the years.

Thank you, Trenton, New Jersey. The outsiders can say what they want about you, but you always made me feel at home. R.I.P Gage.

I learned so many lessons over the few years I went to MCCC, but the biggest lesson I learned was that it's ok to bend but never to break.

CHAPTER 12

Not Bad for a Special Ed Kid

I moved on from Mercer County Community College and decided that I wanted to see if I could get my bachelor's degree. I applied for some four-year colleges. My GPA was almost a 3.0 and my father was doing a lot better at home.

"At this point, if you want to go and try to live on campus, we support you," my mom insisted.

I ended up going to Kean University, and when I got there, I decided that I wanted to play football. I walked on at Kean University and I got a rude awakening that everyone was bigger, faster, and stronger. Those years that I spent away from football, it showed because, yeah, I was fast, but everybody else was, too. Not only that, they were also big and strong.

All the things that I used to get away with in high school, I couldn't do anymore. I had to work on my technique, and I had to basically beat somebody for their spot on the team. I had to work my butt off to make that team. We had to be at spring ball every day at 5:00 a.m. and the weight room right after. I had never put in so much work in my life, but it was all worth it when I made the team. Unfortunately, I didn't cherish the opportunity I had until it was almost taken away. Not just losing my football career, but also my freedom.

After the spring semester ended, I passed all my classes and found out I made the team. I was on cloud nine. I felt like nothing could go wrong…until it did.

Before we left school, coach told me two things. He said, "All right, Moose (which is what he called all Kean football players), when you go home, stay out of trouble and you better keep your weight up."

That brings us to the worst night of my life:

I was home on our break from school, chilling for the summer when a few guys from my block came up with the bright idea that we should drive out to Rutgers and find a party or something. I was bored, so I said sure, why not. I know some girls in that area.

On the way, we made a stop at a park close to the area we were going to. I quickly realized that we stopped so that they could meet up with a drug dealer. It wasn't the first time I was around people that were high before, so I didn't think much of it. I figured I'd play babysitter for the night and make sure everyone got home safely since I was driving.

Soon it became apparent that they were on a different kind of high. Trying to keep them under control made it impossible to communicate effectively and find a place to go. I decided that we would stop looking for a party, go to the main street, and wait for the girls that were coming to meet us.

Soon after arriving, the three guys who came with me befriended an older drunk couple. They all wanted to keep looking for a party. I told them I wasn't in the mood to party; I was going to chill until the girls came. The older guy's girlfriend said she didn't want to walk anymore, so she chose to wait with me until they got back.

Ten or fifteen minutes passed and still no word my guys. I started looking around to see if I could find them, but they were nowhere in sight. As I was walking around, the older guy's girlfriend dropped her purse on the ground. I helped her pick everything up and place it all back inside her purse.

"Thank you," she said.

"No problem," I replied, and kept looking for the other guys.

About five mins later, the three guys came sprinting down the street, yelling, "We gotta go! Now!"

I asked what the rush was about and they said they'd explain when we got home.

We ran to the car and peeled off. As I was driving, I noticed a car following us, then there were cop cars. I said to myself, *I don't know what they did, but I know we are going to jail.* Right after that, the flashing red and blue lights came on and they pulled us over.

Next thing I knew we were surrounded by cops. They told us to drop the keys out the window and put our hands up where they could see them.

They walked up to the car with guns drawn. I glance over my shoulder at my guys and said, "What did y'all do?!" but no one wanted to answer. The police pulled us out of the car and handcuffed us. Then they took us to the police station and impounded my car.

While I was being escorted to the holding cell, the only thing I kept asking myself was, *How did this happen?* I sat in the holding cell for a few hours while they interrogated the other three guys.

As it turns out, the other three were smoking cigarettes dipped in embalming fluid. When the drugs took effect, they performed an armed robbery on the older guy we met. The cops didn't believe me when I said I had no idea what had happened, and they wanted to send me to jail with the rest of them. My only saving grace was that they didn't have anything to pin on me. The girl who stayed behind with me even vouched.

She saw me in the holding cell and said, "Hey, why is he in here? He didn't do anything. He was with me the whole night."

The cops asked her, "Are you sure?"

She said, "Yes, let him go. If he wanted to rob me, he would have done it when I dropped my purse on the ground, but instead he helped me pick everything up and didn't take a thing."

After that, they had to let me go. So they did...at 4:00 a.m. I had to walk home because I had no car and my phone was dead. I walked from New Brunswick to East Windsor—that's a six-hour trek nonstop. When you walk for that long, you have a lot to think about. I was rained on twice, I sang "99 Bottles of Beer" from start to finish four times, and I went through every emotion you could possibly think of.

When I finally made it home, I told my dad what had happened. He said I was lucky that nothing had happened to me and that I needed to be careful about who I hung out with. I spent the next couple of days thinking about how I could have lost everything I worked so hard to get. School, football, my freedom…. Now I completely understood everything my coach at Kean was trying to say.

The head coach of our team was Dan Garrett, probably one of the best coaches I've ever had, hands down, not just because he was a good football coach, he was a great life coach, too. He would encourage us on and off the football field, helping us to become better men. He told us that it goes in this order: faith, family, football. If you keep things in that order, everything will fall into place. He also made sure that we understood the importance of hard work, consistency, and dedication. He made sure that we understood that we're never supposed to be on the football field playing just for self. We should always have the team in mind.

As a team, the word family was an acronym: Forget About Me, I Love You. We maintained that mindset throughout our entire journey together at Kean. He also reminded us that sometimes that 1% more is all you need to put yourself above the competition. He always used to tell us that the boiling point for water is

212 degrees Fahrenheit. I didn't understand it at first, and then he told us the story behind it:

"If the water reaches 211 degrees Fahrenheit, it won't boil. It will never boil. But once it hits 212 degrees Fahrenheit, it boils, and that's all the difference in the world. That 1% more could be the difference between success or failure in your life."

I'm so thankful that I had the opportunity to meet Dan Garrett. He changed my life in ways he'll never understand, and I'll forever be indebted to him and the KU family.

I had a DB coach (a defensive back coach). His name was Coach D'Avanzo. I swear up and down, this man hated me. He hated everything about me. Every day he would constantly yell at me. I don't know what it was, but I felt I could do nothing right in his eyes—ever.

We always had our ball drills at practice on Thursdays, and that was when the defense would work on catching the ball from all different angles. Now, I hated this drill because I have small hands and catching the football was always something I struggled with, and Coach D'Avanzo knew it. When we had our ball drills, I would get in line with all the other defensive backs and one by one we would do our breaks. Zero-degree breaks, 90-degree breaks, 45-degree breaks, and Coach D'Avanzo would throw the ball so damn hard.

For whatever reason, it always seemed like everybody else there was able to catch his passes except for me. But then I realized it was just something I needed to work on. Coach D'Avanzo made me understand that nothing is ever going to be handed to me. He was going to make me earn it. With me being a defensive back, Coach D helped me understand that catching an interception was like the opportunities we often receive in life: When it comes your way, do you let it slip through your hands or do you focus on that opportunity and hold on to it because it has the potential to change everything?

I was a walk-on at Kean University, so I'm not going to tell you I was this all-star player, or that I made this huge difference for the team. No, not at all. It just didn't work out that way for me. Was I talented? Yes. Could I play? Yes. My point is that despite outside circumstances, I was learning to give everything my best effort.

I had a cornerback coach whose name was Coach George Williams. He took a liking to me because he knew how hard I was working. He would help me after practice with my catching skills.

Every day after practice, I'd work on my back pedal with him. He would throw me the ball at different angles, and I'd work on catching it. People would see me staying after practice and laughed, but I didn't care because it was an area where I was weak, and I wanted to turn it into a strength. It took some time to pay off, but then one day we were doing the ball drills at practice. Coach D was throwing passes, firing them left and right. You could hear it coming, smack, smack, smack, tearing up people's hands, but everybody was doing everything in their power to not drop the passes. Dropping passes meant extra conditioning.

In our particular group, the player who had the best hands was Jamahl Williams, our starting free safety. That was my big bro. Anytime I needed help with anything, anytime I had questions, I could always count on big bro to help me out. He was really, really good. Players from other teams used to call him little Bob Sanders because he used to have long dreadlocks and he'd hit anything that was moving. He also had mad ball skills.

When it was my turn for the ball pass, you could hear the players in the back go, "Come on, bro, focus. Don't drop it. Look it all the way into your hands. Don't drop it. You got it. You got it."

On this day, I felt confident. Coach D started throwing the ball, it came in, and I caught it. I go up again for seconds, the ball comes—*boom*! Catch.

"Whoa! He's catching them," one teammate noted.

I go up again, the ball comes, catch.

"Whoa! Okay, something is different. Brad is actually catching these passes."

We finished the entire drill. I didn't drop any passes. This was remarkable because as sure as my name is Brad Butler II, I was going to drop some of those passes. Not all, but definitely some. At least passes coming from Coach D'Avanzo.

The drill was over and our defensive coordinator, Coach Miggz, said, "Which group had the fewest number of drops?"

Unfortunately, it wasn't our group. It was the linebackers who actually dropped the least amount, go figure. Coach Miggz came over to our group and said, "All right. So, who dropped the most passes in this group? Butler, was it you?"

I said, "Nah, coach. I didn't drop any passes."

"Yeah, my ass you didn't drop any passes."

Coach D'Avanzo chimed in. "No, coach, he didn't drop one pass."

I couldn't believe it. I never would have thought Coach D would stick up for me. I didn't think he was going to say anything at all. He said, "Butler, you're getting better." To get a compliment from Coach D'Avanzo meant a lot. Crazy, because at the end of that year, we actually ended up winning an NCAA championship.

I got an NCAA Championship ring. I'm super proud of it, but I don't even keep it for myself. I gave it to my mother because I wanted her to understand that her hard work meant something to me. On awards night, I asked her to come with me. We came in, sat down, and listened to the awards that were given out and, unbeknownst to me, I was called up for the Cougar Award. It's an award given to a defensive player who is a hard worker, someone who had an impact on the team's success.

I remember Coach Dan Garrett saying, "So, for this year, our Cougar Award is going to go to a player who's worked consistently to become a better player every day, and every player knew that when you lined up against him, it wasn't going to be an easy day for you in practice. He wasn't going to let up, and he wasn't going to allow you to get an easy bucket. For that, I want to present our Cougar Award for this year to our defensive back, Mr. Butler Island himself, Brad Butler."

I remember Coach D'Avanzo and Coach George Williams handing me that award. For me, that was a special moment, just all the hard work coming full circle.

In the classroom, I'd pretty much learned when to ask for help. I changed my major to business management because I felt like I needed to learn how to make money and make money work for me. We dealt with so many struggles growing up, and this was a much safer, more legal approach than taking over the "family business." When it came to financials, I wanted to change the trajectory for our family. We didn't have any business owners, so maybe I could be one. The only problem is, I didn't know what I was going to be a business owner of. I didn't really know what my gift was. I had a lot of talents. I can sing. I can dance. I'm a decent athlete. I can draw, but I didn't really know what my gift was.

I fell on some hard times, but I did what I had to do to get through it. I didn't have much money to get back and forth from my house to work and to school. There were a lot of times where I would find an empty parking lot in the middle of the night and I would go to sleep in the back seat of my car in the middle of winter because I couldn't afford a tank of gas. I always kept a blanket in the trunk because I knew those times were going to happen more often than not. I didn't call my mom, and I didn't tell my dad because I didn't want to put more stress on them. Dad's health issues were more than enough.

I spent a lot of nights looking up at the stars, thinking that one day things would get better and I'd never have to sleep in my car again, or go hours on top of hours without eating because I needed to save my money for gas and wait until I was able to get home to eat something. A lot of the students just thought I was an overachiever and that's why I was always at the school as soon as it opened. Nope. I was just trying to hurry up and get out of the cold. And to think after everything I had to go through, I still managed to get my associate's degree in fine arts and a bachelor's in business management from Kean University. Top that all off with an NCAA football championship ring. Ha! Not bad for a special ed kid.

CHAPTER 13
Gifted

After I graduated from Kean University, I started applying for multi-level marketing and sales positions because I wanted to run a business. I tried all these different companies—Amway, Vemma, Legal Shield—you name it. But I realized that I wasn't attracted to the money. I wasn't attracted to the opportunity that the multi-level marketing companies presented. As it turns out, I was actually attracted to the presenter—the person who was presenting the opportunity. I wanted to be on the stage. I wanted to be the guy telling his story to motivate other people, inspiring them, empowering them. Just like my mom did on that audio tape I stumbled upon as a kid.

I'd always had this daydream when I was in school, and I would always get in trouble for it: "Brad, pay attention. Brad, focus. Are you listening? Are you daydreaming again?" I would always have the same daydream that I was standing on the stage with these bright lights shining on me, and a crowd of people watching me. I never knew exactly what I was doing, but I just knew that those people were there to see me. It just took a long time for me to realize that I wanted to be what some would call an effective communicator and/or a motivational speaker, but personally, I like to call it a master storyteller. The first time I'd seen a motivational speaker in person was when I was in high school. They had a gentleman by the name of Dr. Randal Pinkett come and speak to us. He was the first person to win Donald Trump's *The Apprentice*. He stood on that stage and that was the first time that I saw a black man, someone who looked like me and also went to the same school that I was attending, talk about how you could do great things in life—how I, too, could be successful.

Before then, the only people I'd ever seen were white males that were successful in the business world. I lived in the area that was predominantly Caucasian, so all the business owners were white. I didn't see any successful businessmen who looked like me. It wasn't until that point where I started to actually have ideas and thoughts like, *Maybe I could do that. Maybe I could inspire people*. I just didn't act on it until later on in life.

Fun fact: I actually have a picture of Randal Pinkett that he signed, and it says, "To Brad, stay strong, Randal Pinkett." Still have that to this day.

There was a gentleman at my high school. His name was Mr. Napier. One day he stopped me in the hallway and he said, "Brad, you know, you're different from these other kids."

I said, "Okay.

"No, seriously, you're not like these other kids. You have your own way of doing things. You're a leader and you can be whatever it is that you want to be as long as you put your mind to it."

Then he pulled out a piece of paper and a pen and he wrote down on the paper: *The man who says he can and the man who says he can't are both right. Which one will you be?*

I kept that paper and put it in my room and I looked at it all the time. Then later on in life, when I thought about the IEP meetings and all the conversations with my counselors, I read what they wrote about me on the IEP form: *Brad has a learning disability. He's not capable of taking his thoughts and verbalizing them.*

At that point, all I needed to do was put in the time and the effort, be consistent and actually look for a mentor, somebody that could help me. I took some time to myself and went out into the working world to make sure I had some form of income. I got my insurance licenses and started selling. It was all the sales jobs that

I'd had. Once I made the decision that I was going to be a motivational speaker, I quit my job working in insurance and I put all my time and effort into becoming a motivational speaker. I allowed the insurance licenses to lapse because I wanted to put myself in the situation where I couldn't go backwards.

All those years, I convinced myself that because I was in special ed classes that I wasn't going to be capable of telling my story, that I wouldn't be able to verbalize my thoughts correctly. Besides, what made me so special that anybody else would want to hear my story? What gave me the right? What have I done in my life that was so special that I deserve to tell someone else that they can live their dreams?

To help move the process along, I started listening to Les Brown. Then I found Dr. Eric Thomas and he showed me that you could be yourself, that I could be a motivational speaker and I could do it my way. That because there is no blueprint, I could write my own rules. I can write my own story, build my own path.

I had to live by the hashtag that I use—all gas no breaks. That simply means if you have a gift, you must use it as your vehicle to drive you forward and don't take your foot off the gas pedal. For me, it was that simple. I had somebody that told me they weren't quite sure if being a motivational speaker was the best option for me. As I told you before, anytime somebody would tell me that I couldn't do something, it just made me want to do it that much more. Once I'd made up my mind, I started putting all my time and effort into making my dream a reality.

STEP 1—RECONNECT

I needed to build that relationship so that I was able to move by faith and not by sight. I realized that I'd lost my connection to my faith over time. I stopped praying, I stopped giving thanks through the good and the bad. One night while I was laying in bed, dreading going to sleep because I didn't want to have to wake up and go to work at a job I hated, I remember praying, saying to God, "I quit. I submit to your will, whatever it is that you want me to do with my life, please send me a sign. I'm tired of trying to do things on my own; I'm tired of trying to do things my way. I keep messing everything up and you're the only one that can help me fix it.

STEP 2—BECOME WHAT I WANT TO ATTRACT

I said that I wanted to be a motivational speaker. That meant I needed to be a man of character and I needed to uphold values. I had to sit down and really think about the fact that I'm not a man yet. No, I wasn't the worst man in the world, but the fact that I knew there were areas in my life where I was capable of doing much better, and the fact that I wasn't was a real problem. I started to dig deep and ask myself some tough questions. Like, do you value your family? Do you think they made the right choices when you were younger? Should they have chosen different paths? Do you really want a wife? If so, do you really think you're going to find one by club hopping and acting the way you do? Do you really want a family? If you had a child right now, would they be proud to call you their father?

It was a hard lesson to learn, but I knew I'd never see the best version of myself if I kept lying to myself, thinking things would change. The hardest conversation I ever had in my life was the one I had with myself. When I had to look myself in the mirror and say, *"Brad, you're a hypocrite. You say you're a good man, but you're not, look at your track record. You say you want to be successful, but how? You always do the bare minimum. If it's not something within your comfort zone, you give it minimal effort. Men are providers, and you don't provide a thing. Tell me…. Was the lust for money really worth those sleepless nights? You get in your feelings and quit jobs and ghost on people when you don't like the way things are going. You have burned bridges and singlehandedly destroyed relationships because of your pride, arrogance, and childishness. Your family has sacrificed for you time after time and what have you done to show your gratitude? Your ancestors have given their freedom and their lives to grant you the opportunities they only dreamt of having. You have the audacity to complain about the way things are as if you don't live in America, the land of opportunity. You're not a man, you're a scared little boy in a man's body, afraid to face your fears. Are you a man? Nah. But you sure put up a good front."*

STEP 3—PAIN, PASSION, PURPOSE

For so long I ran from the pain, I was always trying to avoid being hurt. For whatever reason, I could never seem to let go. It would replay in my mind over and over and over again. I could talk about all the issues until my face turned blue, but it just wouldn't go away. I still carry the pain of my family and my community on my shoulders. It's a constant reminder that there is more work to be done, that I can't rest until we can live without worries. The pain cuts deep when I see our cities in shambles with drugs and alcohol flooding the streets. People are becoming desensitized to the senseless acts of violence that we see on mainstream media. Fatherless families, so young boys never learn what a real man is.

Babies having babies, trying to raise a child when they are not yet full grown themselves. The pain from the abuse we feel physically, mentally, sexually…. It all stays on my mind and weighs heavy on my heart. I think of those who are drowning in a sea of pain, and I hope that they can just hold on for one more day. I no longer run from the pain. I welcome it, for it fuels my passion. I believe that one day things will change, no matter how dark it gets. It's always darkest right before the dawn. This passion is what wakes me up, what pushes me forward, what won't allow me to quit. This passion I have is something that no amount of money can buy. I speak with passion because I've lived everything that I speak, because I know how far I've come, and I can't go back now. If and when you are lucky enough to find your passion and are able to connect that with your gift, it will lead you to your purpose. When you realize your purpose, you become an unstoppable force. It no longer matters what life has to throw at you because you have made a decision that your purpose is more important than any of that heartbreak and strife. The only thing that matters is making every day count. Making your next day, your best day.

About the Author

BRAD BUTLER II is the CEO and founder of Brad Butler II & Associates, LLC. A motivational speaker and athlete, his goal in life is to motivate, inspire, and empower people all around the world to live their dreams and put forth their best effort in everything they do. Brad, known to his friends as B-Rad, holds a bachelor's degree in business management from Kean University despite being placed in special education classes as a kid.

A few years after graduating from college, Brad discovered his gift of public speaking. He now spends his time traveling from school to school, empowering students and athletes, as well as consulting with companies to train employees on public speaking, leadership development, and team building. Brad's goal is to help others become the best versions of themselves and encourage everyone to take full advantage of their opportunities.

"Make your next day, your best day."

—Brad "B-Rad" Butler II

45893063R00062

Made in the USA
Middletown, DE
25 May 2019